Alum Bay, to the north of the ridge of Downs that terminates at the Needles, is renowned for its soft, eroded cliff made up of nearly vertical strata of coloured sands. Twenty-one different shades of sand can be found which are made up into souvenirs for sale to visitors. A long flight of steps leads down to the pebble beach or the chair lift can be used for easier access to the shore. From the beach boat trips are run to view the Needles rocks and lighthouse and the bay is a popular anchoring place for week-end yachtsmen.

The Needles, perhaps the best known topographical feature of the Island, consist of three pinnacles of chalk some 100 feet high rising from the sea at its western extremity. Originally there was a fourth isolated stack, a slender spire known as Lot's Wife, which fell into the sea in 1764. The famous 80 feet high lighthouse at the seaward end has warned shipping since 1859 when it replaced an earlier structure on the Downs above. Also on the Downs is the fort of the Old Needles Battery, built in 1863 and restored by the National Trust.

Totland Bay (*above*) is a quiet little cliff-top resort complete with a small esplanade, a pier and extensive views towards the Hampshire and Dorset coast. It is also a good vantage point from which to watch the shipping passing in and out of the Western Solent.

Colwell Bay (*below*), adjacent to Totland, consists of a curving sweep of excellent sands which, at low tide, are very extensive, safe and suitable for children. At the northern end is Fort Albert, built in 1856, which faces Hurst Castle across the Solent.

Yarmouth is an ancient town with a busy harbour thronged with yachts and it is the port of entry to the Island for the car ferries from Lymington. Overlooking the harbour is the castle built by Henry VIII and Yarmouth was for many years the seat of the Governor of the Island. The diminutive town is neat and picturesque with a quaint Town Hall, rebuilt in 1763, a church with a very distinctive tower and a 700 feet long pier much used as a promenade and for sea fishing; beside the pier is the clubhouse of the Royal Solent Yacht Club.

Freshwater Bay *(above)* is a little horseshoe-shaped cove eroded out of the chalk cliffs which have been worn away by the wind and waves, leaving isolated stacks to mark the original line of the coast. Beyond the western headland is Tennyson Down *(below)* which rises to an impressive height of 480 feet. Here the poet used to walk each day saying that the air was worth "sixpence a pint". A monument to him stands on the summit of the down.

To the east of Freshwater Bay the road climbs over Afton Down and above the cliffs around **Compton Bay** (*above*). From here it follows the long, low south-western coast, the 'Back of the Island', past Brighstone to Chale and Blackgang Chine.

Freshwater consists of several scattered communities in the centre of the Western Wight peninsula. Here, at Farringford, Tennyson lived for nearly 40 years from 1852. The pretty thatched church of St. Agnes (*below*) was built in 1908 on land given by the poet's son.

Calbourne village lies in the middle of Western Wight. A pretty place, its main attraction is the little lane near the church called Winkle Street (*above*), a long row of stone, thatch and tiled cottages, embowered in flowers, facing a little stream across the grassy verge.

Newtown standing at the head of a now silted inlet was formerly a harbour of some importance, though now it is reduced to a quiet hamlet. A reminder of the town's former position of importance is the Old Town Hall (*below*) which was built in 1699.

Calbourne has possessed a working watermill since at least 1086, when it was recorded in Domesday Book. The present 17th century mill (*above*) still produces stoneground flour. An extension, no longer in use, was added in 1894.

Shorwell (*below*) lies in a sheltered valley on the southern slope of the Island's central chalk down ridge. Like its neighbour Brighstone, it has a number of pretty thatched cottages and a church which dates back to the reign of King Edward III.

Blackgang Chine (*above*) to the west of St. Catherine's Point is a deep cleft in the cliff and was once the haunt of smugglers. Today it is laid out as an adventure park with tableaux, a cowboy village and many other attractions which are illuminated at night.

St. Catherine's Point is the southernmost tip of the Island. The headland and Chale Bay to the west have always been a danger to shipping and the present lighthouse (below) was built in 1838. Inland stands an old light tower built around 1323.

Brighstone is a picturesque village in the south of the Island between Shorwell and Mottistone on the Ventnor to Freshwater road. It has a history dating back to the 9th century when it was given to the Bishoprick of Winchester by King Egbert. Like many of the inland villages of the Island, Brighstone has a charm redolent of old rural England. This is enhanced by a delightful row of thatched cottages known as North Street. With 700 feet high Brighstone Down providing excellent walks and view points and with the sea only a mile away, Brighstone makes an admirable holiday base.

Ventnor is the most southerly of the Island's resorts and is renowned for its balmy climate, being sheltered to the north by the heights of St. Boniface Down, towering over 700 feet behind the town. A steep zig-zag hill leads down from the terraced streets of the Victorian town to the Esplanade and the gently curving sandy beach. At the eastern end is the Canoe Lake overlooked by the Winter Gardens Pavilion, whilst to the west is the extensive Ventnor Park with the Botanic Gardens, a veritable sun-trap with many delightful cliff walks.

Bonchurch which lies immediately to the east of Ventnor is a residential village of winding, tree-shaded lanes in a steeply sloping cliff-side situation. In the middle of the village, near the Victorian church of St. Boniface is Bonchurch Pond (*above*) a small but charming sheet of water embowered in trees and shrubs and the home of water-fowl. From the Pond a narrow lane leads down to the diminutive foreshore. Another hidden lane descends between stone walls to the Old Church of St. Boniface (*below*), a tiny Norman building of great charm.

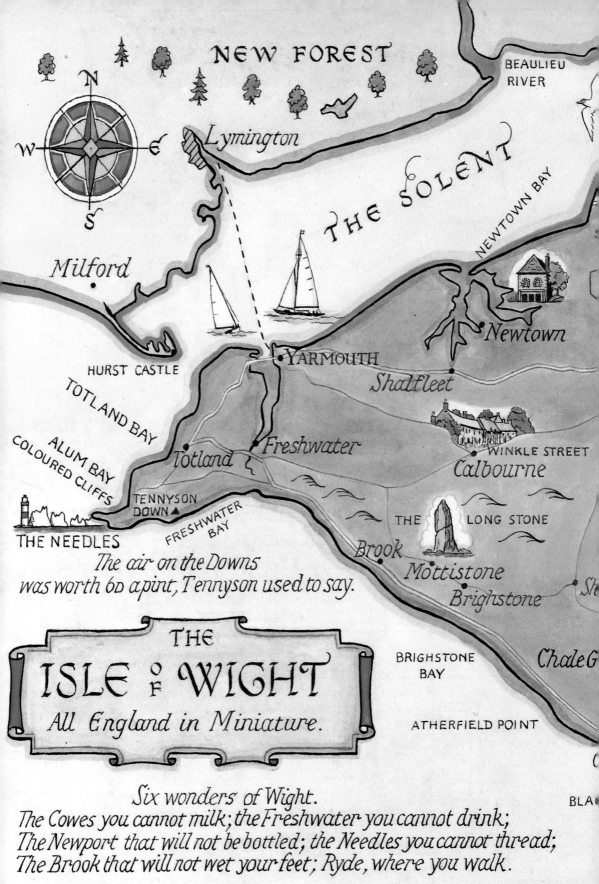

NEW FOREST

BEAULIEU RIVER

N W E S

Lymington

THE SOLENT

NEWTOWN BAY

Milford

Newtown

HURST CASTLE

Shalfleet

TOTLAND BAY

YARMOUTH

ALUM BAY COLOURED CLIFFS

Totland

Freshwater

WINKLE STREET

Calbourne

TENNYSON DOWN ▲

FRESHWATER BAY

THE LONG STONE

THE NEEDLES

Brook

*The air on the Downs
was worth 6d a pint, Tennyson used to say.*

Mottistone
Brighstone

BRIGHSTONE BAY

Ch̲ale G

THE
ISLE ᴼꜰ WIGHT
All England in Miniature.

ATHERFIELD POINT

Six wonders of Wight.
The Cowes you cannot milk; the Freshwater you cannot drink;
The Newport that will not be bottled; the Needles you cannot thread;
The Brook that will not wet your feet; Ryde, where you walk.

BLA

M.F.PECK

ENGL

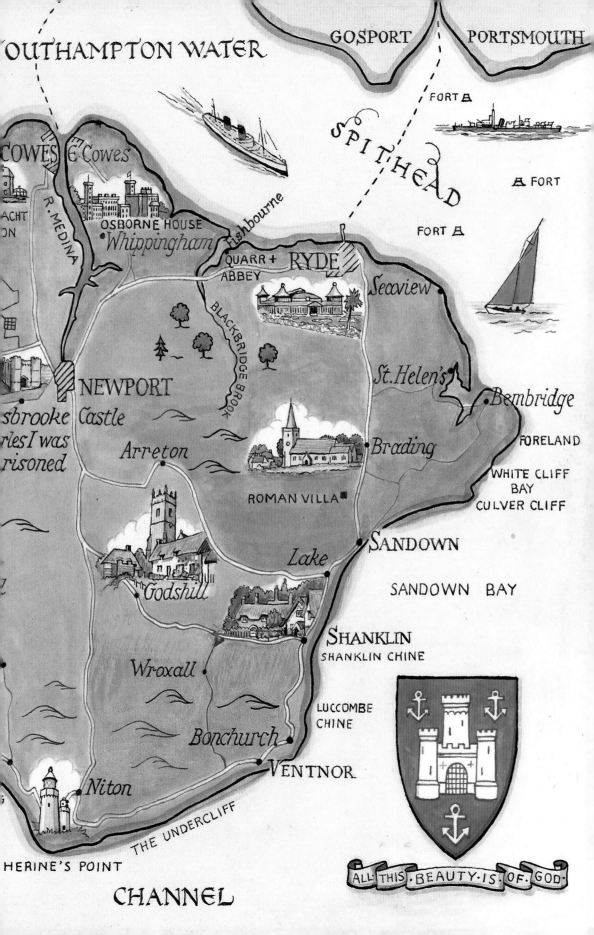

SOUTHAMPTON WATER

GOSPORT PORTSMOUTH

SPITHEAD

FORT ⚓

⚓ FORT

FORT ⚓

COWES E Cowes

OSBORNE HOUSE
Whippingham

R. MEDINA

ACHT
ON

Fishbourne

QUARR +
ABBEY

RYDE

Seaview

St. Helen's

Bembridge

FORELAND

NEWPORT

sbrooke Castle
rles I was
risoned

BLACKBRIDGE BROOK

Arreton

Brading

WHITE CLIFF
BAY
CULVER CLIFF

ROMAN VILLA ■

SANDOWN

Lake

SANDOWN BAY

Godshill

SHANKLIN
SHANKLIN CHINE

Wroxall

LUCCOMBE
CHINE

Bonchurch

VENTNOR

Niton

THE UNDERCLIFF

HERINE'S POINT

CHANNEL

ALL · THIS · BEAUTY · IS · OF · GOD

Shanklin town stands mostly on the cliff top some 150 feet above the sea, whilst the half-mile long Esplanade lies at the foot of a perpendicular wall of rock (above). Access from the town to the shore below is by steep winding roads, by steps and, with less effort, by the convenient Cliff Lift. Situated in the centre of sheltered Sandown Bay, Shanklin with its attractive gardens, bracing cliff-top walks and long safe, sandy beach is one of the most popular resorts on the island. At the southern end of the beach is the bottom of the famous Shanklin Chine,

a deep tree-shaded glen traversed by a winding fern-bordered path. The Chine was cut into the cliff by the little stream which descends from the waterfall at the top to the old, thatched fisherman's cottage far below. Nearby is the Old Village, another of Shanklin's delights. Here thatched and whitewashed cottages and the thatched Crab Inn enclose a bend in the road to Ventnor and transport the visitor, in an instant, from the trappings of a modern seaside town to a picturesque reminder of a bygone age.

Cottages and Church, Godshill

Godshill attracts many visitors to see its thatched cottages along the main street and particularly to admire the delightful group beside the church (*facing*). In the grounds of the Old Rectory there is a fascinating scale model of the village.

Arreton is a rambling village on the road from Sandown to Newport, with a 13th century church of Saxon foundation. Nearby is Arreton Manor (*below*), a splendid Jacobean mansion built in 1612 on an earlier site; it is open to the public.

Sandown lies nearly in the centre of the magnificent sweep of Sandown Bay (*above*) and is renowned for its mile long Esplanade and its extensive and gently sloping sands which are ideal for children (*below*). The town is largely a nineteenth century creation though Henry VIII built a castle here about 1540, second only to Carisbrooke in importance for the defence of the Island. This fortress was washed away by the sea and replaced by Charles I until it too was demolished when the town was laid out. The pier has a modern pavilion and theatre and the High Street

is merely a stone's throw from the shore. To the South is Battery Gardens, a popular vantage point with a good view along the sea front to Culver Cliff whilst in the opposite direction the cliff walk leads past Lake to Shanklin with Dunnose Head beyond (*above*). At the other end of the Esplanade the road to Bembridge passes the Sandham Recreation Grounds, the Children's Canoe Lake covering 18 acres and with water 18 inches deep, a pitch and putt golf course, the sands of East Beach (*below*) and the Sandown Zoo before turning inland behind Bembridge Down.

Whitecliff Bay (*above*) lies on the eastern side of Culver Down, on top of which stands a prominent stone obelisk erected in 1849. The land above the bay is a very popular camping ground and the cliffs here are similar to those of Alum Bay.

Brading (*below*) formerly a port at the head of the eastern River Yar, is a very ancient little town with a church dating from the 7th century. Beside the church stands the Old Town Hall in which are preserved the historic stocks and whipping post.

Bembridge village occupies a site on the Foreland, the easternmost extremity of the Island, spreading from the Harbour to Lane End. The Harbour (*above*) is the estuary of the little River Yar and is a great place for yachtsmen. At the harbour mouth the sands are particularly good and to the North it is protected by the Duver, a spit backed by dunes and grassland preserved by the National Trust. The Trust also cares for Bembridge Windmill (*below*) at the opposite end of the village. Built in 1700, this is the last remaining windmill on the Island.

Newport (*above*) on the River Medina, is the largest town and capital of the Island, being both its shopping and commercial centre. On a hill to the south-west is **Carisbrooke Castle** which dates back to the time of William the Conqueror; the Norman Keep on its high, artificial mound is the oldest part of the fortifications. The imposing Gatehouse (*facing*) leads into Base Court (*below*) in which is the Governor's House, together with the Well House containing the famous donkey wheel. King Charles I was imprisoned in the castle in 1647/48.

The Gatehouse, Carisbrooke Castle

Ryde has been one of the main arrival points for visitors to the Island since the construction of its half-mile long pier (*above*) in 1813 and the establishment of the Steam Packet Service. Today it is the terminal for the hovercraft service from Portsmouth and the promenade is a fine place from which to watch the everchanging procession of vessels in the Solent. With the sandy sweep of Appley Beach (*below*) at one end, the Esplanade is well laid out with pleasant gardens and other amusements for visitors.

The Isle of Wight Steam Railway (*above*) is a working steam railway museum offering passenger rides from Ryde to Wootton. Two of the locomotives were used locally and have been carefully restored to their original livery.

Seaview (*below*) is today officially part of Ryde but it retains its individuality as a charming little holiday resort. It is aptly named for it does have good views across the Solent and is well-known for its sands and sailing facilities.

Osborne House (*above*) near Cowes was built by Queen Victoria and Prince Albert in 1845 as a quiet seaside home for their family. After the Prince's death, in 1861, the Queen preserved the house and grounds unaltered in his sacred memory and she died there in 1901. The Private and State Apartments present a unique and fascinating record of the Royal occupation. Nearby is **Whippingham Church** (*below*) which was designed by Prince Albert and was the Royal Church attended by the family when in residence at Osborne. It contains many Royal monuments.